ISBN: Softcover   978-1-5245-1965-0
       EBook   978-1-5245-1964-3

Print information available on the last page

Rev. date: 02/09/2017

To order additional copies of this book, contact:
Xlibris
1-800-455-039
www.xlibris.com.au
Orders@Xlibris.com.au

DEDICATED TO-

Michelle, Gavin and Christopher.

A most amazing family.

Princess Amber

Written by-
Margaret Wright

Illustrations by —
Kristin Close

Amber was a princess of the very royal kind,
She knew that she was special but she really
                                    didn't mind.
Her home was in a castle in the kingdom of
                                    Wyee,
Where she was the boss of the whole royal
                                    family.

King Gavin was her father and Queen
                                    Michelle, her mother dear,
Her brother Prince CJ brought her so much
                                    cheer.
They reigned over the alpacas, the dogs and
                                    fish galore,
And loved all the visitors who came knocking
                                    at the door.

Amber had a golden web, she'd weave it all
                                    around,
If you were not looking, without a single
                                    sound.
Round and round and in and out, it would give
                                    you quite a start,
Then without the slightest warning, ZAP,
                                    she'd have your heart.

When she turned five as princesses do, she
                              longed to go to school,
It had to be a special place, that was the
                              palace rule.
Gosford East School had such a class of royal
                              princes and princesses,
So off she went to join them in her green and
                              white dresses.

Mrs Wright was so honoured to teach such a
                              class of royal students,
She knew they were very special and definitely
                              heaven sent.
Mr McLeod, the boss of all, would visit to the
                              class and linger,
For those clever princesses would wrap him
                              around their little finger.

A right royal carriage was required to take the
                              princess to school,
Sir Anthony was summoned, he was so very
                              cool.
Assisted by Lady Joanie Pony in the royal
                              limousine,
They were all such a magnificent sight when
                              they arrived upon the scene

A true princess has many angels sent to give
                              her care,
For the one who sends out angels sent Drs
                              Barry and Susie to be there.
They knew much about royal blood and the
                              Special princess's heart,
They worked so hard and did so much, they
                              were very, very smart.

In the royal class was another angel, she was of
                              great delight,
Her name was Nurse Di and she would always
                              set things right.
She was the fastest suctioner in the most
                              amazing places,
Fairy houses, dodgem cars, cruising ships and
                              many running races.

One day, to school, came some lions with huge
                              lion hearts,
They heard about the royal students and
                              wanted to be a part,
Of a team to put together a very special
                              playground,
Where little royals could play and great
                              pleasure would be found.

Royalty calls to royalty and so it was decreed,
That the Governor General of all the land
                              would do a special deed.
To open up the playground for all the land to
                              see,
The royal children played and sang with so
                              much royal glee.

Princess Amber gave her flowers, a very
                              treasured moment,
They talked, giggled and touched noses, a
                              special time sent.
"Come to my Christmas Party at my home in
                              Admiralty House,
It will be so much fun with your friends, no
                              one will ever rouse".

Amber had a special prince, Tom was his name,
They stayed at each other's palaces, it was
                              such a nice game.
They were each other's Valentine and would
                              meet at the movies,
They rode their bikes and walked together,
                              what two royal little groovies.

To distance kingdoms over water, our princess
                    desired to go,
The Lady Kendal was commissioned a most
                    royal yacht you know.
With all the princes and princesses, it was such
                    a royal sight.
For they were pretend sailors and sang sea
                    shanties with all their might.

If you should only think a princess rides in a
                    horse drawn carriage,
Think again for this princess skilfully a horse
                    would manage.
She would stand upon the saddle, she'd trot
                    and ride and spin,
Her special friend Sue from RDA would stand
                    beside and grin.

Gymnastics was another joy our princess would
                    engage in,
She begged to walk on the highest bar, an
                    argument to win.
A master of the trampoline so high she'd make
                    you dizzy,
With a cheeky grin, higher she went it kept
                    Nurse Di so busy.

Those Lions came once again from across the
                              globe,
They cheered and clapped and gave her gifts
                              as on the stage she strode,
'I must away' the princess said, 'I need to be at
                              school',
I love to go each day it is my golden rule".

Homework was a special passion, she couldn't
                              have enough,
It kept Mrs Wright so busy, it was very, very
                              tough.
She so wanted to be a teacher, that's why she
                              worked so hard,
For teachers love to be with children and write
                              their royal report card.

Cooking was another passion she did it for her
                              dad,
King Gavin ate the delicacies, which made him
                              very glad.
Cook Amber donned the apron and very floppy
                              hat,
She mixed the sticky dough and when it went
                              flat you'd hear a royal 'drat'!

It's not well known that princesses love to
                                complete fast running races,
Amber would practice, she'd run and run as
                                she went through her paces.
As fast as the wind, with stick in hand, she'd
                                drive herself to win,
A display of grit and determination, caused
                                heads to be a spin.

Princesses like to trick you as they dress in
                                great disguises,
You look at them and then they change, they
                                give you great surprises.
First a bird, then a nurse, a cook, a lady bird, a
                                queen,
Gardener and bat girl, it created quite a
                                scene.

Many times upon the stage she would revel in
                                her disguises,
For to guess who she was, there were
                                definitely no prizes.
Her famous play, put on the stage, 'Shake Your
                                Tail Feathers',
In black and white she was a delight, achieving
                                her endeavours.

It is the heart of a true princess, to dance
                              upon the stage,
With lights and music, tutus and ballet shoes
                              but first to amaze,
The walking stick (her old faithful friend)
                              simply had to go,
For a princess ballerina works upon her toes.

From far and wide the audience came to see
                              the princess wonder,
In the beautiful lights and friend at side it
                              really made you ponder,
Was this a dance or was it a performance of
                              heavenly grandeur,
Not a dry eye or a life untouched by the
                              display of this beautiful dancer.

With much excitement and joy Amber went to
                              Mr Walsh's scripture lessons,
She learnt of Father God and Jesus her
                              friend in those very special sessions.
One day the bishop came to bless the royal
                              children,
He laid hands on their heads a message of
                              Peace to send.

Amber knew her heavenly home, far more
beautiful than words could say,
Her heart longed to be there and soon
would be the day,

The king of all dominions, her precious Father
God,
Whispered to her spirit, Princess Amber gave a
nod.
"Come my beautiful princess, I have so much
that awaits you,"
She closed her eyes and opened them, it was
all so very true.

Heaven is so beautiful, words cannot describe,
Nana, Sue, Zoe and Leonie were standing at
her side.
They laughed and danced and sang with joy as
they began to play,
Trachi gone, no tubes or pain, no ventilator,
just the perfect way.

Our beautiful princess lives forever and is
very, very able,
To feast on wonderful delights at the King's
banquet table,
School begins with angels and teacher King Jesus,
Everything she has so absolutely pleases.

Princess Amber's story is one of never ending,
She waits in her heavenly home for the time
that is pending.
When you will come to join her in her mansion
in the sky,
She will say "I love you all, will see you bye and
bye."

About the Author

The author has spent many years as a special education teacher in a unit for children with physical disabilities and severe medical conditions. The children there had an amazing zest for life and would relish all that a day at school brought forth. School was fun and provided such a relief from the endless medical appointments and hospitalization. The author gained a master's degree in special education with a qualitative thesis featuring the impact on family life of having a child with a disability. Working closely with parents and families of children with disabilities allowed the author to share in the joys and heartaches these amazing people went through.

There were many opportunities for the author to write stories about the children in the class and read them to the children when they were sad or upset. The children with autism especially responded well to these stories. Laughter was always present and many would create outrageous tricks that would bring even more laughter. A special bond was forged between teacher and family. Parents would ask for the teacher to write special stories about their child when that child lost the battle for life. In that special unit, all knew how to celebrate life, and so there were many times to party and enjoy all that they could do. When new gains were made such as first steps, everyone celebrated, and it was time for a new story to be written.

Edwards Brothers Malloy
Ann Arbor MI. USA
March 31, 2017